BLUEBERRY TOAST
BY MARY LAWS

UK premiere first performed at the Soho Theatre, London on 24 May 2018

CAST

Gala Gordon – BARB
Gareth David-Lloyd – WALT
Adrianna Bertola – JILL
Matt Barkley – JACK

CREATIVE

Writer – Mary Laws
Director – Steve Marmion
Designer – Anthony Lamble
Lighting Designer Rob Casey
Sound Designer – Mic Pool
Fight Director – Bret Yount
Choreographer – Stuart Rogers
Voice Coach – Rebecca Gausnell
Production Manager – Sebastian Cannings
Casting Director – Nadine Rennie CDG
Assistant Director – Lakesha Arie-Angelo
Costume Supervisors – Sarah Mills and Sarah Mercade
Producers for Platform Presents – Isabella Macpherson and Gala Gordon
Producers for Soho Theatre – David Luff and Holly De Angelis

CAST

Gala Gordon – BARB

Theatre credits include: Frida in the premiere of Howard Brenton's *The Blinding Light* directed by Tom Littler at the Jermyn Street Theatre and Irina in Benedict Andrews's acclaimed production of *Three Sisters* at the Young Vic.

Screen work includes: Christine Keeler in Series 2 of *The Crown* for Netflix, Verity in *Endeavour: Arcadia* and Elena in Chris Foggin's independent feature *Kids In Love* opposite Will Poulter and Cara Delevingne.

Gareth David-Lloyd – WALT

Theatre credits includes: *Cat on a Hot Tin Roof* (Theatr Clwyd); *The Stick House* (Raucous); *Twelve Angry Men* (Kenwright); *Lyre, Oscar and Jim* (HighTide Festival); *Three Women and a Piano Tuner* (Chichester/Hampstead Theatre); *Twelfth Night* (English Touring Theatre); *After Agincourt, Before Nell* (L&G Productions) and *The Threepenny Opera* (National Youth Theatre).

Television and film include: *The Widow, Albert, Robin Hood: The Rebellion, Waterloo Road, Dark Signal, Holby City, Red Faction, Warehouse 13, Torchwood, Sherlock Holmes, Girl Number 9, A Very British Cover Up, Caerdydd, Doctor Who, Beethoven, The Bill, Rosemary and Thyme, Absolute Power, Casualty* and *Mine All Mine.*

Adrianna Bertola – JILL

Theatre credits include: Markie/Lily/Tina/Little Girl in *The Twilight Zone* (Almeida Theatre); Violet Beauregarde in *Charlie and the Chocolate Factory* (original cast Theatre Royal, Drury Lane); Matilda in *Matilda* (original cast, RSC); Young Cosette in *Les Miserables* (Queen's Theatre); Gretl von Trapp in *The Sound of Music* (London Palladium) and Brigitta von Trapp in *The Sound of Music Anniversary Tour* to Kuala Lumpur, Malaysia.

Film credits include: *Nativity 2: Danger in the Manger.*

Television credits include: Sharice in *Casualty, Silent Witness, Hank Zipzer, Call the Midwife, Red or Black, Mr Eleven, The Erin Simpson Show, The Little House, The Harry & Paul Show, Doctors, Magic Grandad.*

Recordings Include: *Matilda* (original cast album recording), *The Sound of Music* (cast album recording).

Other work includes: Mini Jessie J in the *Who's Laughing Now* music video, performed live at V Festival with Jessie J, various commercials including *Littlewoods, Compare the Market, Hyundai, BT, Batchelors* and various voice over work including *Disney, MTV* and *Microsoft.*

Matt Barkley – JACK

Matt trained at Mountview Academy of Theatre Arts and New York Film Academy. Theatre credits include: *Gangsta Granny (West End/UK Tour).* Short film credits include: *The Soup* (The Forum) and *Alien Culture* (BFI/London Calling).

CREATIVES

Mary Laws – Writer

Mary is a native of Texas and received her MFA in playwriting in 2014 from the Yale School of Drama. Mary's plays include: B*ird Fire Fly*, *The Drive* and *Wonderful* (Tympanic Theatre Company); *What A Very Pretty Pageant!* and *Stand (an autumn play)* (The American Laboratory); *The Trapeze Artist* (Baylor University) and *This* (Yale Cabaret). Her work has been read/developed by Baylor University, Theater Masters National MFA Playwrights Festival, the American Laboratory, Rattlestick Playwrights Theater, the Endstation Theatre Playwrights Initiative, Le Pavé d'Orsay in Paris and The Horton Foote American Playwrights Festival. For three years she served as literary associate at Rattlestick Playwrights Theater in New York.

Film/television includes: *The Neon Demon* (dir. Nicolas Winding Refn, Cannes Film Festival selection, released by Amazon Studios) and three seasons writing and producing *Preacher* (AMC).

Awards include the Howard Stern Scholarship and UR/SA Grant for Playwriting. She mentored for the Yale/Co-Op Eugene O'Neill Playwriting Program, the Dwight/Edgewood Project in New Haven and taught Playwriting at Wesleyan University. She received her BFA from Baylor University.

Steve Marmion – Director

Steve is artistic director of Soho Theatre. Since joining Soho Theatre he has directed: *Roller Diner* (winner of the West End Wilma Award for Best Comedy 2017); *Bits of Me Are Falling Apart; First Love is the Revolution; Death of a Comedian* (co-production with Lyric Belfast and Abbey Dublin); *I Kiss Your Heart; The One* (returning summer 2018); *The Night Before Christmas; Address Unknown; Pastoral; The Boy Who Fell Into A Book; Utopia; Fit and Proper People; Mongrel Island* and *Realism*. In March 2016 he directed the new musical *Only the Brave* (Wales Millennium Centre). Since December 2015, he has written and directed *Jack and the Beanstalk, Cinderella* and *Aladdin* at the Oxford Playhouse. Prior to joining Soho Theatre, Steve directed *Macbeth* for Regent's Park Open Air Theatre and *Dick Whittington, Aladdin* and *Jack and the Beanstalk* for the Lyric Hammersmith. In 2009 he directed the highly successful production of Edward Gant's *Amazing Feats of Loneliness* for Headlong Theatre, which received rave reviews at Soho Theatre. In 2008 he had three critically praised successes with *Vincent River* in New York, the original Edinburgh production of *Only the Brave* and *Metropolis* in Bath. He also transferred Rupert Goold's *Macbeth* onto Broadway. Steve was assistant, then associate director, at the RSC for over two years from 2006-07. In 2004 he directed several premieres for Sir Alan Ayckbourn at the Stephen Joseph Theatre and returned to direct the Christmas show in 2006. He has worked with the National Theatre, RSC, in the West End, on Broadway, at the Royal Court, Lyric Hammersmith, Theatre Royal Plymouth, Theatre Royal Bath, Watford Palace Theatre, Sherman Theatre Cardiff and Edinburgh Fringe Festival. *Only the Brave*

(2008) was nominated for Best New Musical and Best New Music at the MTM: UK Awards, and his *Madam Butterfly's Child* (2004) and *Mad Margaret's Revenge* (2005) won the London One Act Theatre Festival.

Anthony Lamble – Designer

Credits at Soho Theatre include: *Roller Diner*, *First Love is the Revolution* and *The One*.

Further theatre credits include: *Again*, *Hamlet* and *Boa* (Trafalgar Studios); *Jack and the Beanstalk* (Oxford Playhouse); *Twiststorm* (Park Theatre); *Run The Beast Down* (Finborough Theatre); *The Inn at Lydda* (Shakespeare's Globe); *A Month of Sundays* (Queen's Theatre, Hornchurch); *The Bastard of Istanbul* (Istanbul International Theatre Festival); *Joe Lycett* (Live Recording at Duchess Theatre); *Hamlet Who's There* (Elsinore Shakespeare Festival); *Allegro, Cyrano de Bergerac, Three Sisters* and *Shivered* (Southwark Playhouse); *Test Rock Opera* (Scala Basel); *Pygmalion* (Vienna's English Theatre); *Richard III, Clarion, Shrapnel: 34 Fragments of a Massacre* and *Ghost From A Perfect Place* (Arcola); *The Devil Masters* and *Spoiling* (Stratford East); *Ciara, The Artist Man and Mother Woman* and *The Arthur Conan Doyle Appreciation Society* (Traverse Theatre); *Peter Pan and the Designers of the Caribbean* (Bloomsbury); *The Tempest* (RSC/Ohio); *Omeros* and *Romeo and Juliet* (Globe Theatre); *Charlie F* (UK Tour/Toronto); *Jackie The Musical* (Gardyne Theatre, Dundee); *Shush, The Passing, The East Pier, Bookworms, The Comedy of Errors* and *The Playboy of the Western World* (Abbey Theatre, Dublin); *For Once* (Pentabus); *Relatively Speaking* (Watermill); *The Complaint* and *Everything Is Illuminated* (Hampstead); *The Price* (West End/Tricycle/Tour); *The Caucasian Chalk Circle, Translations, Sing Yer Heart Out For The Lads, A Midsummer Night's Dream* and *As You Like It* (National Theatre); *Measure For Measure, Richard III, The Roman Actor* and *King Baby* (RSC), *The Entertainer* (Old Vic).

Film credits include: *Pond Life* (Open Palm Films).

Dance and opera credits include: *Facing Viv* (English National Ballet); *L'Orfeo* (Japan Tour); *Palace in The Sky* (English National Opera) and *Broken Fiction* (Royal Opera House).

Rob Casey – Lighting Designer

Credits include: *The Grinning Man* (Trafalgar Studios); *Silver Birch* (Garsington Opera); *Old Vic Gala* (The Brewery); *National Theatre Gala* (Olivier, National Theatre); *Messiah* and *King Lear* (Bristol Old Vic); *Ariodante* and *Giove in Argo* (Britten Theatre); *The 25th Annual Putnam County Spelling Bee* and *Honk!* (GSA); *I and the Village* (Theatre503); *Sister Act* (Yvonne Arnaud Theatre); *Ravi Shankar Workshop* (Linbury Theatre, Royal Opera House); *The Music Man* (ArtsEd); *Payback* (Riverside Studios); *These Shining Lives* (Park Theatre); *Ignition* (Frantic Assembly); *Rigor Mortis* (Finborough Theatre); *Misery* (Bournemouth Pavilion) and *Betwixt!* (Trafalgar 2).

Mic Pool – Sound Designer

Mic's West End and Broadway credits include: *Witness for the Prosecution* (County Hall); *Art* (West End/Broadway/Old Vic/Worldwide); *Fortunes Fool* and *No's Knife* (Old Vic); *Brand* and *Breakfast at Tiffany's* (Haymarket); *The King's Speech* (Wyndham's); *The Postman Always Rings Twice* (Playhouse); *The Madness of George III* (Apollo); *The Unexpected Man* and *The Hound of the Baskervilles* (Duchess); *When We Are Married* (Savoy); *Dr Faustus* (Fortune); *The 39 Steps* (Criterion Theatre/Worldwide, Tony Award for Best Sound in a Play for the Broadway production).

Other work includes: *The Captain of Kopenick* (National Theatre); *A Midsummer Night's Dream, The Seagull, Victoria, Beauty and the Beast* and *The Roundhouse Season of Late Shakespeare Plays* (RSC); *Kathleen Turner – Finding My Voice* (The Other Palace); *Dial M for Murder* and *The Graduate* (West Yorkshire Playhouse/UK Tours); *Gaslight* (Royal Theatre Northampton); *Deny, Deny, Deny* (Park); *Silver Lining* and *The Real Thing* (ETT); *Beryl* (WYP/UK Tours/Rose); *Single Spies* (Rose Theatre, Kingston); *The Stopping Train* and *Overworlds and Underworlds* (Gavin Bryars); *Smoking with Lulu, The Night Before Christmas* and *Roller Diner* (Soho); *Our Country's Good* (Out of Joint); *Touched, Faith Healer* and *Restoration* (Royal Court); *You Never Can Tell, The Ice Chimney* and *Summer with Monika* (Lyric Hammersmith); *Shockheaded Peter* and *Rambert Dance Company* (International Tours).

Bret Yount – Fight Director

Recent theatre credits include: *Nine Night* (Dorfman, NT); *Cyprus Avenue* (Abbey Theatre, Dublin); *Br'er Cotton* (Theatre503); *Caroline or Change* (Hampstead Theatre); *The Twilight Zone* (Almeida); *Goats* (Royal Court); *Hedda Gabler* (NT Tour); *Fanny & Alexander* and *A Christmas Carol* (Old Vic); *The Exorcist* (Phoenix Theatre); *Hamlet* (RADA/KBTC); *Girl from the North Country* (Old Vic/Noel Coward); *Gloria* (Hampstead Theatre); *The Treatment* (Almeida); *The Resistible Rise of Arturo Ui* (Donmar Warehouse); *The Cardinal* (Southwark Playhouse); *Who's Afraid of Virginia Woolf* (Harold Pinter); *An American in Paris* (Dominion Theatre); *The Miser* (Theatre Royal Bath/Garrick Theatre); *Midsummer Nights Dream* (Young Vic); *Bubbly Black Girl Sheds Her Chameleon Skin* (Theatre Royal Stratford East); *Experience* (Hampstead Theatre Studio); *Raising Martha* and *LUV* (Park Theatre); *The Children, X* and *Linda* (Royal Court Downstairs); *Lazarus* (King's Cross Theatre); *One Night in Miami* (Donmar Warehouse); *The Mountaintop* (Young Vic); *King Lear* (RSC); *They Drink It In the Congo* (Almeida); *Strife* (Minerva, Chichester); *La Boheme* (Opera Holland Park); *Don Carlo* (Grange Park Opera); *Romeo and Juliet, The Painkiller, Red Velvet* and *The Winter's Tale/Harlequinade* (Garrick Theatre – KBTC); *Observe the Sons of Ulster Marching Towards the Somme* (Headlong); *Only the Brave* (Millennium Centre, Cardiff); *Ma Rainey's Black Bottom* (National Theatre); *The Caretaker, The Master Builder* and *The Hairy Ape* (Old Vic); *Bad Jews* (Theatre Royal,

Bath/Haymarket); *Cyprus Avenue* (Abbey Theatre, Dublin/Royal Court Upstairs); *Primetime, Human Animals, I See You* and *Violence and Son* (Royal Court Upstairs); *Private Lives* (ATG Tour); *Waiting for Godot, Romeo and Juliet* and *The Effect* (Sheffield Crucible); *The Winter's Tale* (Cheek by Jowl); *The Wasp* (Trafalgar Studios); *First Love is the Revolution* (Soho Theatre); *Hamlet* (Barbican); *Richard II* (Globe Theatre); *Tipping the Velvet* (Lyric Hammersmith) and *Medea* (Gate Theatre).

Stuart Rogers – Choreographer

Stuart trained at Laine Theatre Arts. Choreography work includes: *Peter Pan* (Venue Cymru Llandudno /QDOS); *Day, month, second* (music video for GIRLI); *Remember Remember* (new musical workshop, Stratford East); *Roller Diner* (Soho Theatre); *Late Night Gimp Fight* (Soho Theatre/Edinburgh Festival); *Club Mexicano* (new musical workshop); *The West End Experience* (UK Tour); *Bare* (The Finsbury Town Hall); *Cinderella* and *Jack and the Beanstalk* (Oxford Playhouse); *Cinderella* (Harlequin Theatre); The Stylophones album launch at the Leicester Square Theatre; The Stylophones *Confidential Encounters* music video.

Assistant choreographer on *Strictly Come Dancing* and various corporate and trade shows for major brands.

Rebecca Gausnell – Voice Coach

Rebecca is a freelance voice and dialect coach. Theatre includes: *The Inheritance* (Young Vic, dir. Stephen Daldry); *Killer Joe* (Trafalgar Studios, dir. Simon Evans); *Fiddler on the Roof* (Liverpool Everyman, dir. Gemma Bodinetz), *A View from the Bridge* (Tobacco Factory Bristol, dir. Mike Tweedle); *Fool for Love* (Found 111, dir. Simon Evans) and *Chicago* the musical in the West End. Television includes: *Doctor Who* (BBC), *Endeavour* (ITV), *Plebs* (ITV2) and *Berlin Station* (Paramount Pictures TV).

Film includes: *Waiting for Anya* (dir. Ben Cookson), *If Beale Street Could Talk* (dir. Barry Jenkins) *Tau* (Netflix) and *The Widow* (dir. Neil Jordan).

Rebecca also teaches in drama schools around Europe including Central, Fontainebleau School of Acting, and Arts Ed. She holds an MFA in Voice Studies from the Central School of Speech and Drama and a BA from Northwestern University in Chicago.

Sebastian Cannings – Production Manager

Sebastian is a graduate of the Central School of Speech and Drama. He joined Gary Beestone Events & Theatre as assistant production manager for *Harry Potter and the Cursed Child*. Now supporting all areas of the business, recent production credits as PM include *Around the World in 80 Days* for Kenny Wax, *Wilde Creatures* for Tall Stories and *Buggy Baby* for The Yard Theatre. Seb is trained in IOSH Managing Safely, CIEH Level 2 Award in Fire Safety Principals and Emergency First Aid at Work. Sebastian is working on *Blueberry Toast* for Gary Beestone Events & Theatre.

Nadine Rennie CDG – Casting Director

Nadine has been casting director at Soho Theatre for over fifteen years, working on new plays by writers including Dennis Kelly, Vicky Jones, Phoebe Waller-Bridge, Roy Williams, Philip Ridley, Shelagh Stevenson, D. C. Moore, Alecky Blythe and Oladipo Agboluaje. Directors she has worked with during this time include Rufus Norris, Tamara Harvey, Indu Rubasingham, Michael Buffong, Paulette Randall, Tim Crouch, Natalie Ibu, Roxana Silbert and Ellen McDougall. Freelance work includes BAFTA winning CBBC series *DIXI* (casting first three series). Nadine also has a long running association as casting director for Synergy Theatre Project and is a full member of the Casting Directors Guild.

Lakesha Arie-Angelo – Assistant Director

Lakesha is Soho Theatre's resident director having assisted on *Touch* by Vicky Jones and the 2015 Verity Bargate winning play *Roller Diner* by Stephen Jackson. Previous directing credits include: *Alive Day* (Bunker Theatre for Pint Sized Plays); *AS:NT* (Theatre503 as part of Rapid Write); *Prodigal* (The Bush Theatre for 'Artistic Directors of the Future Black Lives: Black Words') and scratch of *Sugar, Rum, Molasses* (The CLF Theatre) as writer and director. As resident assistant director at Finborough Theatre: *P'Yongyang*, *Treasure* and Vibrant 2015 Festival of Finborough Playwrights. During the residency, Lakesha was awarded the Richard Carne Trust sponsorship.

Isabella Macpherson for Platform Presents – Producer

Isabella started her career at M&C Saatchi, going on to become publisher, then editor-in-chief of ArtReview Magazine. Since 2003, Isabella, through production companies she co-founded – Arts Co and A&B Productions – has produced critically lauded projects across art, theatre, short film and fashion, with a particular emphasis on rising star talent. Isabella is a strategic advisor to the BFC Fashion Trust, the British Film Institute and a trustee of/plus ambassador for The Bush Theatre.

Soho Theatre is London's most vibrant venue for new theatre, comedy and cabaret. We occupy a unique and vital place in the British cultural landscape. Our mission is to produce new work, discover and nurture new writers and artists, and target and develop new audiences. We work with artists in a variety of ways, from full producing of new plays, to co-producing new work, working with associate artists and presenting the best new emerging theatre companies that we can find.

We have numerous artists on attachment and under commission, including Soho Six and a thriving Young Company of writers and comedy groups. We read and see hundreds of scripts and shows a year.

'the place was buzzing, and there were queues all over the building as audiences waited to go into one or other of the venue's spaces....young, exuberant and clearly anticipating a good time.' Guardian.

We attract over 240,000 audience members a year at Soho Theatre, at festivals and through our national and international touring. We produced, co-produced or staged over 35 new plays in the last 12 months.

As an entrepreneurial charity and social enterprise, we have created an innovative and sustainable business model. We maximise value from Arts Council England and philanthropic funding, contributing more to government in tax and NI than we receive in public funding.

Registered Charity No: 267234

Soho Theatre, 21 Dean Street
London W1D 3NE
Admin 020 7287 5060
Box Office 020 7478 0100

Supporters

Mary Laws

BLUEBERRY TOAST

OBERON BOOKS
LONDON

WWW.OBERONBOOKS.COM

First published in 2018 by Oberon Books Ltd
521 Caledonian Road, London N7 9RH
Tel: +44 (0) 20 7607 3637 / Fax: +44 (0) 20 7607 3629
e-mail: info@oberonbooks.com
www.oberonbooks.com

A catalogue record for this book is available from the British
Library.

PB ISBN: 9781786824790
E ISBN: 9781786824806

Cover image: Roo Kendall for Artroom

Printed and bound by 4EDGE Limited, Hockley, Essex, UK.
eBook conversion by Lapiz Digital Services, India.

For Dustin Wills
My Texas Love
Who first brought this play to life.

Production History

Originally produced by the Echo Theater
Company, Los Angeles, California
September 17th – October 24th, 2016

Tympanic Theatre
Athenaeum Theatre, Chicago, Illinois
February 13th – March 13th, 2016

Yale School of Drama
Iseman Theater, New Haven, Connecticut
November 8th – November 10th, 2012

Characters

WALT

BARB

JACK

JILL

Setting:

Walt and Barb's beautiful, sunny kitchen. The kind that has
a breakfast area attached. The kind with a small sitting area,
too, with a loveseat. The kind that might have an upright
piano and a window seat draped in baby blue and yellow
lace, wouldn't that be heaven?! The kind of kitchen where
you will make hot meals that will nourish your family, where
lively conversation is sent reverberating down the hallways,
where board game nights meet corny "dad jokes" and low-
fat ice cream sundaes meet homemade hot fudge. The kind
of kitchen with kindergarten drawings that are framed,
not slapped half-heartedly on the brand new stainless steel
refrigerator. Oh, what a marvelous kitchen!

A Note About Sound:

I like the idea of a full thirty seconds to a minute of sound
before the play begins. In blackness in the theater. The sound
of a neighborhood street. A car honks. A bicycle bell dings.
An ice cream truck drives by and we hear excited squeals of
neighborhood children running to get a Drumstick or a clown-
shaped popsicle with a bubble gum nose. A man's voice calls
out, "Boys! Come inside."

Lights up on WALT and BARB's sunny kitchen and living area.

WALT is sitting at the breakfast table reading papers.

He scribbles furiously and wickedly with red marker.

BARB enters.

BARB: Good morning, dear.

WALT: Good morning, dear.

BARB: Lovely Sunday morning.

WALT: It is, dear.

    It's a lovely Sunday.

BARB: Have you had breakfast?

WALT: Not yet, dear.

BARB: What can I get you?

WALT: Don't trouble yourself, dear.

BARB: You need to eat.

WALT: I'm not hungry.

BARB: You look hungry, dear.

    WALT scribbles furiously.

BARB: You look ran-vuss.

    More scribbling.

BARB: Practically ran-vuss!

WALT: You mean ravenous, dear.

BARB: Okay.

    WALT scribbles.

    BARB whimpers.

    He scribbles more.

    She whimpers more.

WALT: Alright.

BARB: Wonderful!

    What can I get you?

WALT: Let me think.

BARB: Anything in the world!

WALT: Anything?

BARB: Anything your heart desires.

WALT: Well, now.

    I'll have to think about this.

BARB: Take your time, dear.

WALT: Anything in the world?

BARB: Anything your little heart desires!

    He thinks.

WALT: Hmmm.

    Let me think.

    He thinks.

WALT: Hmmm.

    He thinks harder.

WALT: Hmmm.

    Anything at all?

BARB: Anything your little teeny tiny heart desires.

WALT: Hmmm.

    Hmmmmmm.

    He is very still.

    He's a statue.

BARB: Have you thought of something, dear?

WALT: Blueberry toast!

BARB: Blueberry toast?

WALT: Blueberry toast!

> That sounds divine this morning!
>
> Blueberry toast!

BARB: Coming right up!

> *She begins making blueberry toast.*

WALT: How did you rest?

BARB: I slept well.

> Very well.
>
> That new mattress!

WALT: I know!

BARB: It's a dream!

WALT: That's the real stuff.

BARB: It ought to be

> After what we paid.

WALT: Worth every cent.

BARB: But, Walt!

> Two thousand dollars for a mattress!

WALT: So?

> The Parkinsons bought the King Plush with the foam topper.
>
> Now that's a real waste.

BARB: How do you know that?

WALT: I saw it.

BARB: When?

WALT: The other day.

BARB: But what were you doing at the Parkinsons?

WALT: I saw it outside, dear.

BARB: Why was their mattress outside?

WALT: It was being unloaded, dear.

Off the van.

BARB: What kind of van?

WALT: What do you mean
    What kind of van?

BARB: Was there a logo?

WALT: On the van?

BARB: Yes, for the store.

WALT: I can't recall.

BARB: I was wondering where Kathy ordered the mattress.

WALT: It just looked like a plain white van.
    But I could tell from the packaging
    King Plush with the foam topper.
    And I know what *that* cost them.

BARB: Was Kathy there?

WALT: When?

BARB: When you saw them unloading the mattress.

WALT: Hmmm.
    I can't recall.

BARB: She wasn't helping?

WALT: No.
    It was just a bunch of Mexicans.

BARB: Oh, my.

She hands him a plate of blueberry toast.

WALT: What's this?

BARB: It's breakfast.

WALT: But what is it?

BARB: Blueberry toast.

WALT: Blueberry toast?

BARB: Yes.

Blueberry toast.

WALT: I've never heard of such a thing.

BARB: But

WALT: Blueberry *toast?*

BARB: That's what you said you wanted, dear.

WALT: I most certainly did not.

BARB: You did.

You did.

I said

Anything you want.

And you said

Anything in the world?

And I said

Anything your teeny tiny little bity itty little heart desires.

And you said

Blueberry toast.

WALT: I said blueberry *pancakes.*

Blueberry toast isn't a thing.

BARB: But I made it a thing.

Look

I mixed a little honey and lemon into the blueberries

Like a compote.

WALT: Well that's a disgusting word.

BARB: What word?

WALT: That one.

BARB: Compote?

He clears his throat.

He holds out the plate.

WALT: I'd like blueberry pancakes, please.

BARB: Your tone

WALT: No.

Barb.

Do not start that, Barb.

You said anything I wanted.

I want blueberry pancakes.

She takes the plate.

BARB: Coming right up.

She throws the blueberry toast into the garbage.

She sends him a small, ever-so-subtle look as the toast makes a dramatic "thunk" into the trashcan.

She begins making blueberry pancakes.

WALT: Hmmm.

BARB: What's that, dear?

WALT: Oh, nothing.

Some student assignments.

Listen to this

'All the faces of innocence

Were welcomed in her youthful one

And in her gaze

I felt relief.'

BARB: That's lovely.

WALT: What does it mean?

BARB: What *does* it mean, Walt?

WALT: You tell me, Barb.

I swear.

These kids.

WALT scribbles furiously with the red marker.

BARB: I think it's romantic.

>Teaching a poetry class.

>I would like to teach a poetry class.

>*WALT laughs.*

BARB: What's so funny, Walt?

WALT: It's just

>You know nothing about poetry, dear.

BARB: I still think it's romantic.

>Just the way it sounds.

>Poetry.

>Poetry class.

>Poetry.

>Poooetry.

>I'm teaching a

>Poooetry class.

>Lovely.

WALT: I ought to get into oil.

>That's where the money is these days.

BARB: But, Walt

>What about the young minds?

WALT: The young minds can educate themselves.

>Oil.

>That's where the gold is.

>Get some of that Iraqi oil

>Maybe open up a string of gas stations

>That's the life, Barb.

BARB: If you say so, dear.

>*JACK and JILL enter.*

JILL: Daddy!

>Daddy!

WALT: Well, hello, Jilly Bean!
　　How's my Jilly Bean today?

JILL: I'm awake, Daddy!

WALT: You are, little Jilly Bean.
　　I see that.

JACK: Good morning.

BARB: Good morning, Jack.

WALT: Morning, son.

JILL: Daddy!
　　Can you guess what we've been doing?

WALT: Just now?

JILL: Yes!
　　Just this morning, Daddy!

WALT: Are you building a rocket?

JILL: No!

WALT: Are you skinning a cat?

JILL: No, Daddy!

WALT: Are you pirating the Pacific?

JILL: We're writing a play!

WALT: A play?

JACK: Yes, a play, father.

BARB: That's wonderful, children.

WALT: What will your play be about?

　　JILL giggles.

JILL: We can't tell you, Daddy!

JACK: You'll have to wait and see.

JILL: Come on, Jack.

Let's go figure out the costumes!

The children run out.

WALT: Sweet kids.

How did we have such sweet kids, Barb?

BARB places a plate of blueberry toast on the table in front of him.

WALT: What's this, dear?

BARB: Blueberry toast.

WALT: Blueberry toast?

BARB: Yes.

WALT: I thought we discussed this, Barb.

BARB: I felt you needed another chance.

WALT: Another chance?

BARB: Yes.

WALT: Another chance for what?

BARB: See

I went back into the kitchen to make blueberry pancakes

After you said you didn't want to try my blueberry toast

With the honey-lemon compote

WALT: Watch your mouth, Barb.

BARB: And halfway through heating up the pan

I thought

He didn't even try my blueberry toast.

I worked so hard to make it

And he didn't even try it.

So I thought I would give you another chance.

Take a bite.

WALT clears his throat.

WALT: Barb.

BARB: Yes, dear.

WALT: I'm not sure what has come over you, Barb.

BARB: Just a little bite.

A tiny bite.

WALT: I don't want to take a bite.

I don't need another chance to try your blueberry toast

To know

That I don't like blueberry toast.

BARB: But *how* do you know?

WALT: Because I know.

See right there

Where the blueberry

BARB: Compote?

He clears his throat.

WALT: Yes.

Right there where it is touching the toast.

BARB: Yes.

WALT: See how it's a little soggy underneath?

BARB: It's not too soggy.

WALT: I don't want soggy toast, Barb.

Or see here

Where there are no blueberries at all

BARB: You could spread them over

With a knife!

She grabs a knife.

WALT: I don't want dry toast, dear.

BARB: Try spreading the blueberries.

She holds out the knife.

WALT: I don't want to spread the blueberries.

BARB: Here.

Just give a little spread.

WALT: I'm not interested in spreading.

BARB: Would you like me to spread for you?

WALT: BARB!

WOULD YOU PLEASE STOP WITH YOUR
INCESSANT NAGGING!

BARB raises the knife, slightly.

She smiles.

She takes the plate of blueberry toast back to the kitchen.

She begins making blueberry pancakes.

WALT checks his wristwatch.

WALT: It's getting late.

BARB: Do you have to be somewhere today?

WALT: I do.

BARB: But it's Sunday, Walt!

WALT: I promised the Parkinsons I would help mend their
sliding glass door.

BARB: What happened to their sliding glass door?

WALT: I assume it shattered.

What do you mean what happened?

BARB: I'm not asking what happened.

I'm asking how.

WALT: Tim fell through it, dear.

BARB: Through the door?

WALT: Right through the door.

BARB: Oh!

Poor little Timmy!

JACK enters.

JACK: Mother.

Do you have a bunch of carrots?

BARB: A bunch of carrots?

JACK: Yes.

The long kind

With the leafy stems.

BARB: What do you need the carrots for, Jack?

JACK: For our play.

WALT: Give them the moon

And they ask for a dollar.

BARB looks in the refrigerator.

BARB: I don't have carrots.

I have mushrooms.

JACK: No.

BARB: I have cabbage.

JACK: Cabbage?

WALT: Esch, cabbage!

I hate cabbage.

Why do you always buy cabbage?

JACK: What does the cabbage look like?

BARB holds up a head of cabbage.

WALT: Take the cabbage for your play, Jack.

JACK: I'll take the cabbage.

BARB: Are you sure?

WALT: Take the cabbage, Jack.

JACK takes the cabbage and exits.

BARB: Is he okay?

WALT: Who?

Jack?

BARB: No, Timmy Parkinson.

WALT: He's been in the hospital for a day, Kathy said.

BARB: You talked to Kathy?

WALT: Yes, but she said he would be fine.

Just a concussion.

Very minor.

BARB: When did you talk to Kathy?

WALT: The other day.

BARB: Which other day?

WALT: I don't remember.

BARB: When they were unloading the mattress?

WALT: Yes.

That must have been it.

BARB: I thought you said Kathy wasn't there.

WALT: Did I say that?

BARB: You did.

You did.

Just like you said you wanted blueberry toast for breakfast.

WALT clears his throat.

WALT: I have an obligation, Barb.

Please hurry, if you're so inclined.

Please hurry with the pancakes.

BARB begins mixing batter, furiously.

JACK and JILL run in.

They are dressed in various mismatched clothing they either wore for Halloween –

Or found in their parents' closet.

JACK holds the cabbage.

JACK: Would you like to see the first act?

WALT: The play has more than one act?

JILL: Yes!

It has four!

WALT: Four?

JILL: Yes!

WALT: Do plays usually have four acts?

JACK: Ours does.

JILL: Will you watch, Mommy?

BARB: I would love to, sweetie

But I'm hurrying.

I'm too busy hurrying to watch your play.

JILL: Alright.

JACK: The first act is called

Wrestling With Suburbia.

WALT: Wrestling With

Now where did you hear that?

JILL: We made it up!

WALT: That's a pretty grown-up thing to make up.

JACK: Jill!

Get in your spot.

JILL gasps and ducks under the table.

JACK prepares.

JACK: I am Jack.

    Jack I am.

    That's my name.

    The one I was born with.

    Born from a long line of carrot salesmen.

JILL: Pst.

    Jack!

JACK: What?

JILL: It's cabbage now.

JACK: What?

WALT: It's cabbage now, Jack.

JACK: Born from a long line of cabbage salesmen.

    JACK yawns dramatically.

JACK: Boy, I sure am tired and thirsty.

    Been walking around this town all day selling my cabbage.

    Where oh where could I find a glass of water?

    JILL rolls out from under the table.

JILL: Ah!!!!!!!

    I'm a pirate!

    I will destroy you!

JACK: Oh, no, not a pirate!

JILL: Give me all your money!

JACK: I have no money!

    Only this last cabbage.

    It's all I have in the world.

JILL: All in the world?

JACK: All in the world.

JILL: I'll take it!

She takes it.

JACK: Who are you?

JILL: My name is Federico Gonzago Rodrigo Flamingo
     Sticky Ketchup Monkey Bottom
     Boom-Boom Kitty-Kitty Applesauce.
     Who are you?

JACK: I'm Jack.

They shake hands.

JACK: Can I have a glass of water, Federico?

JILL: Sure okay.

She pantomimes handing him a glass of water.

He drinks it.

JACK: Ah!
     Much better!

They bow.

WALT claps.

WALT: Bravo!
     Bravo!

JILL: Did you like the first act, Daddy?

WALT: I loved it, Jilly Bean.

JACK: Come on, Jill.
     Let's go rehearse the song.

JILL: Okay, Jack!

The children exit.

WALT: What an odd play.
     What does it mean?
     I swear
     These kids.

BARB tosses a plate of blueberry toast on the table.

WALT stares at it.

BARB: It's blueberry toast.

WALT: I see that.

BARB: I want you to eat it.

I want you to eat my blueberry toast.

WALT: Barb.

BARB: I want you to eat it.

I want you to try my blueberry toast.

It's very good.

I had a bite in the kitchen.

WALT: Barb.

BARB: Please try it, Walt.

Try the blueberry toast.

Eat the toast!

Eat the toast, Walt.

EAT THE TOAST, DEAR!

WALT stands, probably for the first time.

He picks up the blueberry toast.

He walks to the trashcan.

He drops the entire plate of blueberry toast into the garbage.

It makes a dramatic "thunk".

BARB's heart breaks.

BARB: You're a cunt.

WALT and BARB stare at each other.

WALT: Barb!

BARB: Why wouldn't you just try it, Walt?

What is so wrong with blueberry toast?

WALT: I told you what was wrong with it, dear.

BARB: But you didn't even try it.

    You didn't even try!

WALT: How dare you call me a cunt, Barb.

    Barb?

    What gives you the right to call me a cunt, Barb?

BARB: I just think you're acting like one.

WALT: I think you're acting like a bitch, Barb.

    I think you're acting like a royal fucking bitch

    But I don't go around saying it.

BARB: Well, maybe you should.

WALT: I don't think that's an appropriate thing to say.

BARB: I think it is.

    Perhaps we should start saying what we think.

WALT: That's no way to live.

BARB: Perhaps you should tell me when you think I'm acting

    Like a royal fucking bitch

    And I'll tell you

    When you're acting like a complete fucking asshole!

WALT: That's a dangerous game, Barb.

    WALT and BARB stare at each other.

WALT: Fine.

    You know what I think?

    I think that when I wake up

    On a lovely Sunday morning

    And I say

    I would like some blueberry waffles

    I would like you to make me

    Some BLUEBERRY FUCKING WAFFLES!

BARB: Waffles?

WALT: Yes!

Waffles!

BARB: Pancakes!

WALT: I meant pancakes!

BARB: Pancakes are different than waffles!

WALT: Well I wouldn't know!

I don't see any pancakes *or* waffles!

All I see is blueberry toast!

Blueberry toast!

Everywhere I look it's

BLUEBERRY FUCKING TOAST!

BARB: WHAT IS SO WRONG WITH BLUEBERRY TOAST!?!?

WALT: It's revolting.

BARB: You're revolting!

WALT: Look!

Look!

Here's the pancake mix!

Right here.

He throws the box of pancake mix at her.

WALT: And let's see.

He opens the fridge.

WALT: We have plenty of eggs.

He tosses the eggs on the counter.

WALT: And what else do we need?

BARB: We need a lot of things.

WALT: Ah, milk.

Here's the milk!

He holds up the milk.

WALT: And look!

Syrup!

Blueberries!

All the ingredients are right here in the fridge, dear.

Right here in the fucking fridge, dear.

BARB: Your tone

WALT: No.

Don't start that, Barb.

BARB: But why do you talk to me like that?

WALT: You said to say what I'm thinking.

BARB: You act like I'm a total moron.

WALT: Then stop being one, Barb!

It's very simple.

BARB: You always do that.

You always act like I'm a total moron.

BARB begins to cry.

WALT: Oh, here we go.

BARB: Leave me alone.

WALT: Here come the waterworks.

BARB: Leave me alone, Walt.

WALT: Such a victim.

You're such a victim, Barb!

BARB: I SAID LEAVE ME ALONE!

BARB cries out.

She runs at WALT and lunges for his throat.

He pushes her away.

She picks up the carton of eggs.

She begins to throw eggs at him.

BARB: Leave me alone, Walt!

Leave me the fuck alone, Walt!

WALT: Goddammit, Barb.

BARB: I just wanted you to eat the toast.

WALT: I didn't want your cunting toast!

BARB: Would it have been so hard to eat the toast?

WALT: Barb!

There's egg all over the floor.

BARB: That's because I've been throwing eggs at you, dear!

WALT: Someone's going to slip on an egg.

BARB: I hope it's you!

And I hope you break your neck!

I hope you break your fucking neck on an egg, dear!

WALT slips on an egg.

He falls on the floor.

BARB: Walt!

BARB runs to him.

WALT groans.

BARB: Darling, are you alright?

I'm so sorry.

I'm so sorry about the eggs!

I should never have thrown the eggs at you.

Are you okay?

She kneels over him on the floor.

BARB: Walt.

Talk to me, Walt!

Are you okay?

WALT: I'm okay.

BARB: Oh, thank god.

WALT: I'm alright.

BARB: I thought you fell and broke your neck.

WALT: I didn't break my neck.

BARB: What would I do without you, Walt?

What would I do if you fell and broke your neck?

WALT: Life would go on, dear.

BARB: No.

No.

Life would end.

Life wouldn't go on.

WALT: Could you get me a towel, dear?

BARB: Of course.

She gets a towel.

BARB: Would you like me to dampen it?

WALT: A dry towel is fine.

BARB: Perhaps I should just dampen a corner.

WALT: It's fine like that, dear.

Please just bring it to me.

BARB: I'll just dampen the corner.

She dampens the corner.

She brings him the towel.

WALT: Thank you, dear.

He wipes the egg off of his foot.

BARB: Is that better?

WALT: Better.

Yes.

BARB: I'm so sorry, Walt.

I don't know what came over me.

WALT: You shouldn't let your emotions take control.

BARB: I know.

She starts to cry.

WALT: There, there.

Everything's fine.

See?

He rolls his head around and around.

WALT: Nothing's broken but eggs.

BARB: Sometimes I feel like *I'm* broken, Walt.

WALT: You're not broken, dear.

BARB: Are you sorry you married me?

WALT: Of course not, dear.

BARB: Are you sorry you married such a witch?

WALT: You aren't a witch, Barb.

BARB: I just called you a cunt, though.

Don't you remember that?

WALT: Of course I remember it, dear.

BARB: You do?

WALT: It only happened a minute ago.

BARB: I hoped you would have forgotten already.

She sobs harder.

WALT: There, now.

Don't cry.

BARB: You are sorry you married me, aren't you?

23

WALT: Barb.

   You know what I did the day I married you?

BARB: What did you do?

WALT: I bought a gun.

BARB: A gun?

WALT: Yes.

   I bought a gun and I hid it in the third drawer of our dresser.

BARB: With your sweaters?

WALT: Tucked inside my purple sweater.

   Just folded right inside.

BARB: Is it there now?

WALT: It is.

BARB: Is it loaded, Walt?

WALT: It is loaded.

BARB: Why did you buy a gun, Walt?

WALT: Because I was going to shoot you, Barb.

BARB: You were?

   You were going to shoot me?

   She sobs buckets.

WALT: I was.

BARB: Why would you shoot me, Walt?

WALT: There, now.

   It's not for the reason you think.

BARB: Why were you going to shoot me?

WALT: Because I loved you so much.

   I loved you so much, Barb.

   I felt helpless against the powers of the world.

   I felt

If anything ever happened to you
What would I do?
You were so beautiful on our wedding day
With those flowers pinned back in your hair
What were those called?

BARB: Gardenias.

WALT: Gardenias.

Gardenias pinned back in your hair.
All the faces of innocence pressed into your face.
Into you in a white dress.

BARB: Like the poem?

WALT: What poem?

BARB: Like the poem from before?

WALT gets up.

He picks up the poem from the table.

WALT: 'All the faces of innocence
Were welcomed in her youthful one
And in her gaze
I felt relief.'
Ha!
These kids.

She sobs.

WALT: Why are you crying now, dear?

BARB: Because you bought a gun.

WALT: I did.

BARB: Because I was like the poem.

WALT: Does that make you cry?

BARB: That's such
That's such a wonderful thing to do!

WALT: It was.

BARB: You were going to shoot me!

WALT: I was.

BARB: Oh, Walt.

She goes to him.

BARB: I love you, Walt.

They kiss.

He kisses down her neck.

He begins to unbutton her blouse.

WALT: You smell like blueberries.

BARB: Oh, Walt!

He throws her violently onto the table.

He rips the clothing from her body.

They begin to groan and grunt like animals.

JACK and JILL enter.

JILL gasps.

WALT: Oh!

Hello, Jilly Bean.

JILL: What are you doing to Mommy?

JACK: They're copulating.

BARB: Jack!

JILL: What's copulating?

WALT: It's like wrestling

BARB: When you love the person you're wrestling with.

Only when you love the person.

JILL: Oh.

JACK: We finished the second act!

WALT: Bravo!

Let's see it.

JACK: Jilly.

Get in place, Jilly.

JILL is still staring at her near-naked parents.

JACK: Jill!

Shut your trap and let's go already.

JILL: Sorry!

JILL gets into place.

Perhaps she stands on a chair.

JACK sits at the piano.

JACK: Ready?

JILL: Ready.

JACK: This act is called

The Dark and Humble Joys of Mankind.

BARB: Oh!

How lovely!

Isn't that lovely, Walt?

JACK begins plunking out notes on the piano.

JILL sings, very animatedly gesturing and moving to the song.

JILL: *(Singing.)*

OH I AM A GIRL

AND I AM A TREE

I AM AN APE

AND I AM A BEE

I AM A BREATH

AND I AM THE RAIN

LA LA LA LA

LA LA LA LA LA

    LA LA LA LA

    LA LA LA LA LA!

    AND ONE DAY I'LL DIE

    AND NO ONE WILL CRY!

    JACK plays a virtuosic and haunting solo on the piano.

JILL: *(Singing.)*

    LA LA LA LA LA!

    LA LA LA LA LA!

    JACK stands.

    The children take a bow.

WALT: Bravo, children!

BARB: Bravo!

    Very moving!

JACK: Come on, Jill.

    Let's go write the third act!

JILL: I can't, Jack.

WALT: What's wrong, Jilly Bean?

JILL: I feel so sad.

BARB: Because of the song?

    JILL nods and blubbers.

WALT: Don't cry, Jill.

    My little Bean.

JACK: She's been crying all morning.

BARB: She has?

JACK: I told you, Jill.

    It's just the facts of life.

    We've all got to die someday.

JILL: But no one will cry!

WALT: Perhaps.

   Perhaps no one *will* cry.

JACK: Come on, Jill.

   Get it together.

   The children exit.

BARB: Poor dear.

WALT: She'll be fine.

BARB: Would you cry, Walt?

   If I died would you cry?

   If you had shot me on our wedding day

   Would you have cried?

WALT: Perhaps I would have, dear.

   But we'll never know.

BARB: Because you didn't shoot me.

WALT: Exactly.

BARB: Are you glad you didn't shoot me, dear?

WALT: Have you seen my belt?

BARB: It's right here, dear.

WALT: Ah!

   Thank you.

   He dresses.

WALT: Well, I better be off.

BARB: Where are you going?

WALT: To the Parkinsons.

   To mend their sliding glass door.

BARB: Oh, yes.

   Poor little Timmy.

   How *did* he fall through that door, I wonder?

WALT: He'll be fine, dear.

Don't worry.

BARB: I hate sending you off on an empty stomach.

WALT: I'm not hungry for breakfast, dear.

BARB: But what about your blood?

WALT: What about my blood, dear?

BARB: Your blood will go down if you don't eat.

WALT: You mean blood sugar, dear?

BARB: Okay.

WALT: My blood sugar is sufficient.

She whimpers.

WALT: Please, Barb.

She whimpers again.

WALT: I could go in a few minutes, I guess.

BARB: Really?

WALT: If you'll make me some of your special blueberry pancakes.

Could you do that?

BARB: I guess I could do that.

WALT: Could you, dear?

It's been a very trying morning.

I could use a stack of those blueberry pancakes.

I really could.

BARB: Sit down.

Sit right there and don't move a muscle.

He sits.

She goes to the kitchen and makes blueberry pancakes.

WALT plays with the red marker.

WALT: She's such a strange little girl, isn't she?

BARB: Who?

Jill?

WALT: I think her head is halfway in the sky sometimes.

BARB: I think she's alright.

WALT: Of course you do, dear.

BARB: What does that mean?

WALT: It means what it means.

BARB: She's sensitive.

She's a poet.

WALT: I don't care for poets.

BARB laughs.

WALT: Why are you laughing?

BARB: Because you teach poetry, dear.

And you say you don't care for poets.

Or poetry at all!

WALT: I don't.

The world isn't sunshine and rainbows.

Poetry's a waste.

You have to walk boldly and loudly through life

Or you'll be trampled to death.

BARB: Trampled by what?

WALT: By fate, perhaps.

By the wind.

By other people.

By anything really.

BARB: Is that really what you think, Walt?

WALT: It is.

BARB: I had no idea you were such a pessimist.

WALT: Ask anyone.

    They'll tell you the same.

    I ought to get into oil.

    That's what I ought to do.

    I was talking to Kathy about it the other day

BARB: Kathy Parkinson?

WALT: Yes, Kathy Parkinson.

    Do you know another Kathy, dear?

BARB: No, I suppose not.

WALT: Kathy thinks so, too.

BARB: Thinks what, dear?

WALT: That I should go into oil

    Aren't you listening?

BARB: I'm trying to listen, dear.

    I feel a bit distracted.

    All of a sudden

    Distracted

WALT: She thinks this is the time to do it.

    There's plenty of oil in the Middle East.

    Of course I don't speak the language.

    But that's manageable.

    I suppose I could hire a translator

    Or I guess I could learn

    But that's such a bother.

    Oh, well.

    That's what you have to do sometimes.

    At least that's what Kathy says

    BARB smashes a plate of blueberry toast onto the table.

She holds a knife to WALT's neck.

BARB: Eat the toast.

WALT: What the fuck, Barb!?

BARB: Eat the toast.

WALT: I don't want the toast.

BARB: Eat the toast or I'll slit your goddamn throat, Walt.

> This is me
>
> Walking boldly and loudly through life
>
> And I am boldly saying
>
> EAT THE TOAST OR I'LL SLIT OPEN YOUR THROAT!
>
> I'LL GASH OPEN YOUR WINDPIPE
>
> AND SHOVE IT INTO YOUR HEART!

WALT: Who are you kidding, Barb?

BARB: What?

WALT: You aren't going to slit my throat, dear.

BARB: I have a knife at your neck, Walt.

> And I intend to hold it here until you eat the toast.
>
> Eat the toast, Walt!

WALT: No!

BARB: Eat the fucking toast, Walt!

WALT: Never!

BARB: Eat the motherfucking toast, Walt!

> I swear!
>
> I swear I will cut your good-for-nothing throat, Walt.

WALT: You won't.

> I know you, Barb.
>
> You won't do it.
>
> And I won't eat your revolting fucking toast.

A suspended moment.

BARB finally releases his neck.

She drops the knife to her side.

WALT stares at her with a knowing grin.

Suddenly:

BARB grabs his hair.

She jerks his head back –

And slits a small, fast, furious cut onto his throat.

WALT: SHIT!

BARB: I said I would do it.

WALT: MOTHERFUCKING FUCK!

BARB: Oh, does it hurt, Walt?

WALT: YOU CUT MY THROAT, BARB!
YOU CUT MY FUCKING THROAT.
JESUS CHRIST!

BARB: Does it hurt?

WALT: YOU FUCKING BITCH!
OF COURSE IT HURTS.

BARB: Would you like a towel, Walt?

WALT: FUCK YOUR TOWEL AND GO TO HELL!

BARB: It's not too deep, is it?
I tried not to cut too deep, Walt.
I really did.

WALT clears his throat.

BARB: Here.
Take this towel.

BARB grabs a towel and dampens the corner.

She brings it to WALT.

WALT: I don't want your towel.

BARB: Take it.

Take the towel, dear.

You're bleeding.

WALT: I see that, Barb.

BARB: You're bleeding, Walt.

I forgot you had any blood.

WALT: Don't you think I see that I am bleeding?

Don't you think I see that?

It's because you cut my throat, Barb!

BARB: I did.

WALT: You cut my throat.

BARB: I did.

WALT: I can't believe that you cut my throat.

BARB: I told you that I would.

In fairness, Walt.

I gave you fair warning.

WALT: When is it ever fair to cut someone's throat, dear?

BARB: I think it's sometimes fair.

WALT: Name one time.

BARB: Right now.

WALT: Yes, dear.

Right now.

Name one time when it is fair

When it is appropriate to cut another person's throat.

BARB: Right now.

WALT: Yes!

Jesus Christ!

Right now.

Name one time right now!

What did you think I meant, next Tuesday, dear?

BARB: Alright, dear.

…

Perhaps when someone does something you don't like.

When someone has been doing something you don't like for some time.

Then perhaps it's fair.

When someone is blind to your needs

Purposefully blind

When it is as though they have pulled out their eyes

Their own eyes

So there are only dark foreign sockets

And they no longer look human.

Or

When someone cares more about a mattress than sex

Or

More about going than staying

Or

Perhaps when you're drowning

You've been drowning for ages

But you JUST WON'T DIE!

And the only way

The only way to get the smallest breath of air is to cut

Just a little cut

Into the throat of the ocean which is drowning you

So that the water cries out

And a red wave pushes you up up

Just barely

Up

And you catch a glimpse of a gull
Flying above
A white gull waving to you, crying, "Mercy! Mercy!"
And
Oh!

WALT: What *are* you going on about?

BARB: I don't exactly know.

WALT: Hand me that towel.

BARB: Here you are, dear.

She hands him the towel.

He blots his wound.

WALT: I really don't understand what has come over you,
Barb.

BARB: I don't either.

WALT: I'm very concerned.

Are you feeling well?

BARB: I feel wonderful, dear.

WALT: You're very flushed.

BARB: Am I?

WALT: You're very red.

You're nearly blue, dear.

Nearly purple!

BARB: Yes, I can feel all my blood!

I forgot I had any in me at all!

Then I saw yours

WALT: And you're speaking in the strangest way.

BARB: Yes, I can feel my tongue!

I can taste all the words in my mouth.

They taste wonderful!

37

> WONDERFUL.
> WONDERFUL WONDERFUL!
> WALT.
> WOOONDERFUL, WAAALT!
> POOETRY, WAAALT!
> COMPOTE, WALT!
> COOOOOMPOOOOTE!

WALT: Barb.

BARB: YEEES, WAAALT?

WALT: Barb.

Did you dampen this towel?

BARB: What?

WALT: Did you dampen this towel?

He waves the towel furiously.

BARB: I suppose I did.

WALT: You suppose?

BARB: I suppose I dampened the corner, dear.

WALT: Why did you do that?

Why did you dampen the corner?

BARB: I don't know.

WALT: Of course you do, dear.

BARB: Well, I suppose because it helps.

When you're wiping something off of something else.

Like egg

Or blood

It helps to have one corner just a little bit dampened.

WALT: It's revolting, Barb.

It feels revolting against my skin.

BARB: It's just a little moist.

WALT: That's a disgusting word, Barb!!

BARB: What word?

Moist?

WALT stands and goes to leave.

WALT: That's it.

I've had it, Barb!

I've simply had it.

You will not listen to me!

You simply will not listen!

It's a very unattractive quality in a woman, Barb.

The inability to use one's EARS.

Those little flaps of flesh that bookend the hollow hard of your skull.

I am your HUSBAND, Barb.

You are legally BOUND to me.

As I am BOUND to you, Barb.

As I am BOUND to you.

I feel I have given you a good home, Barb.

A proper home for the life you said you wanted.

Two children.

Plenty of money.

Look at our life, Barb.

Look at these curtains.

Look at this fridge!

You could fit a body in here!

A whole person's body, Barb, right in our fridge!

Isn't that the greatest thing you've ever seen?

BARB: It's remarkable.

WALT: Yet you insist on dampening my towels.

You refuse to make me the breakfast I request.

BARB: But you asked for

WALT: No Buts, Barb.

    You refuse to listen.

    And so you know what I am going to do?

BARB: What are you going to do, Walt?

WALT: I am going to cross the street to Kathy Parkinson's house

    Where I will help mend their sliding glass door

    But first, Barb

    First I will ask her to use a dry towel

    A clean, dry towel for my throat, Barb.

    And I will ask her for breakfast.

    Perhaps she'll make me some eggs.

BARB: Eggs, Walt?

WALT: Perhaps.

BARB: I've not heard you say a word about eggs, Walt!

WALT: That's because you don't listen, dear.

    That's exactly my point, dear.

BARB: How do you like your eggs, Walt?

WALT: I suppose I like them sunny side up.

BARB: You like them very runny, Walt?

WALT: I like to pop the centers, Barb.

    It gives me great pleasure to pop the centers.

BARB: I could make you eggs, Walt!

WALT: You've had your chance to make me eggs.

BARB: But

    You never said you wanted

WALT: Please just stop nagging, Barb.

    It makes my throat throb.

    My throat is THROBBING, Barb.

    YOU CUT MY THROAT.

I'm going to get a dry towel

And I'm going to press it to my throat

And I'm going to TRY AND STOP THE THROBBING!

He starts to leave.

She runs to block his path.

BARB: Wait!

Wait, Walt!

Please wait!

Don't leave yet, dear.

I don't want you to leave.

I can make you eggs!

I can make the best eggs!

So runny, Walt.

So moist!

He starts to leave again.

BARB: WAIT!

I didn't mean

I meant

SILKY.

WALT: Silky?

BARB: Yes, dear.

I make the silkiest eggs.

I don't know why I haven't made them for you before.

How silly of me, really.

How stupid!

I am so stupid, Walt.

You make me so stupid because I love you so much.

Please.

Eat my eggs!

Let me make you eggs!

They're so silky smooth
They slide right down your throat.
You don't even have to swallow, Walt!
Just open your throat and

She makes a slurping noise.

BARB: They slide right down!

WALT: Now that sounds very interesting, Barb.

BARB: Does it, Walt?

WALT: Why haven't you made eggs for me before?

BARB: There are a lot of things I haven't made you, Walt.

WALT: Is that so?

BARB: It is so.

WALT: It is so?

BARB: Mmm-hmm.

WALT: Soooooooooooo

He pulls her to him.

She definitely still has the bloody knife in her hand.

He begins chewing on her neck.

BARB: Oh, Walt!
Walt!
You're an animal!

He makes animal sounds.

He pulls at her clothing with his teeth and growls.

BARB: Walt!
Walt, dear!
You're getting blood on my dress!

WALT: Where?

BARB: Right here.

She touches her breast.

He howls.

She runs the tip of the knife playfully down his chest.

He turns her around violently.

He twists her knife-arm behind her back.

He breathes in her ear.

He slaps her hard on the backside.

She winces.

He slaps her again, a little harder.

He holds her down on the ground until she submits.

He looks quite proud.

WALT: Now let's see these eggs.

BARB: You just sit right down, Walt.

Just sit right here and relax.

He sits.

BARB looks for the eggs.

WALT sighs.

BARB does not notice.

She realizes she has run out of eggs.

WALT clears his throat.

He sighs again.

A big dramatic sigh.

BARB shoots him a smile.

WALT: Now this is the life, Barb.

This is the life I've always dreamed of!

I barely notice my throat anymore.

BARB: That's wonderful, dear.

WALT: Don't get me wrong, I haven't forgotten all about it.

But it feels somehow

Less.

BARB: Less is good, Walt.

It is!

That's what they say, anyway.

WALT: What, dear?

BARB: They say less is good!

WALT: Less is MORE, dear.

BARB: Okay.

And more is good.

WALT dabs at his neck with the towel.

The dry end, of course.

WALT: You really are quite stupid, Barb.

There's no use skirting around it at this point.

You've always been quite stupid, Barb.

And you should know that I married beneath me.

Everyone thinks so.

They say it out loud, even.

Why, just the other day when I went to the market

When I went to pick up the things that *you* had forgotten

I overheard someone saying it.

Poor Walt.

Poor Old Walt.

Growing older every day.

He had such potential, that Walt.

Such aspirations.

Now?

He teaches poetry to pimply-faced middle-schoolers.

He's washed up!

Poor poor Walt.

Poor Walt.

And all because he married beneath him.

That's what they say.

I don't mind telling you now, dear.

And I have to endure it.

I have to walk through their thorns as they rip at my exterior.

I have to hold my head up.

It's very hard, Barb.

The external pressures of this world.

It can be very disappointing, dear.

Very disappointing.

But I don't expect you to understand.

You don't have to deal with the things I deal with.

And I deal with them on a day-to-day basis, Barb.

A day-to-day basis.

And you know what?

No one even notices.

You don't see anyone throwing me a parade when I feed not one

Not two

Not three

But *four* mouths.

Four mouths.

Three meals a day.

That's twelve meals a day, Barb.

Twelve!

You know what that is?

It just occurred to me!

You know what that is, dear?

That's every last fucking one of the disciples of Jesus Christ.

Jesus fucking Christ!

And I didn't see him feeding them hamburgers or scrambled eggs.

You know what they ate, Barb?

Thin little pieces of bread.

Like tortillas but not even as good.

Unleavened fucking bread that they dried on rocks in the sun.

Because they didn't have Baking Soda, Barb.

Because they didn't have *money* for Baking Soda.

So in a way, it's all about perspective.

It's really about how you look at things.

And about where you are in your heart.

Your Personal Stability.

And I have to say

I am quite content, Barb.

Look at my hands.

Steady as a rock.

And I'm a good neighbor, too.

I help our neighbors cut their grass and mend their sliding glass doors.

And sometimes when I go through the drive-thru, I pay for the person behind me.

I pay for their meal or their coffee.

And that makes me feel like a good person, Barb.

It makes me feel content.

Like I am doing my part.

And if I can just get into oil.

If I can just get into that Iraqi oil.

He makes a sound like sucking air through his teeth.

WALT: Then life will be something.

Really, truly something.

I think I will be able to meet my maker and say

Yes!

I did everything I set out to do.

I made the best of my talents and abilities.

I provided for my family.

Because I don't mind telling you now, dear

We aren't all going to Heaven.

The Christians will.

And the Jews, of course.

They are the Chosen People, after all.

And maybe a few really conservative Unitarians.

But not the ones who smoke pot for religious reasons.

That's just not decent.

Neither is cutting someone off in traffic.

Those folks are definitely

He whistles and points his finger downwards in a motion indicating "They are going to Hell."

WALT: As are all the feminists.

The single mothers.

Social smokers.

Social drinkers.

It's all or nothing, is what I always say, dear.

The Democrats.

The foreigners.

Construction Workers!

Liberalists.

Abortionists.

Idealists.

Accompanists.

Really anyone with an 'ist' I think.

Don't get me started on the 'isms'.

How did I get started in the first place?

Oh, dear.

What was I trying to say?

Look at me getting overly excited!

I feel so light, Barb.

Such relief!

Such relief!

And, oh!

Would you look at that?

My wound is already filling with pus.

Wasn't that quick, Barb!

I've always been advanced.

My mother would say, "There goes Walt, my very *advanced* little boy!"

Did you know that she breastfed me until I was *eleven*?!

Eleven years old, and it didn't affect me in a negative way in the slightest.

Not in the slightest, dear.

If anything it grounded me.

I mean

Look at these hands!

Steady as a rock.

It doesn't even matter that I married beneath me.

These hands!

These hands!

He holds out a hand, flat and steady, and he admires it.

BARB is standing behind him.

WALT has not noticed.

BARB is holding the bloody knife.

In the other hand, she is holding an exceptionally tall stack of blueberry toast.

A suspended moment as WALT admires his hands and BARB stands poised behind him.

BARB gently slides the toast onto the table in front of WALT.

WALT looks at the toast.

He exhales, knowingly.

He raises his head and gazes at the world of nothing in front of him.

In BARB's hand, the knife rises higher and higher.

WALT: Barb?

And higher and higher.

WALT: Barb.

What is this, Barb?

And higher.

Poised perfectly.

WALT: Is this

He clears his throat.

WALT: Is this blueberry toast?

Barb?

Am I seeing blueberry toast?

Barb?

Dear?

Would you say that I would be correct

In saying

That this is a plate of blueberry toast.

On the table.

In front of me.

Barb?

Barb!

Barb?

Silence.

WALT: Barb?

BARB screeches like a hawk.

A war cry.

WALT winces and curls inward, bracing himself.

BARB goes to stab WALT in the back, but just as the knife is about to pierce his flesh –

JACK and JILL run in.

JACK is carrying a stereo.

JILL gasps!

WALT and BARB freeze.

They turn their heads to the children.

No one moves.

JILL: Mommy?

No one moves.

JILL: Mommy, what are you doing?
What are you doing to Daddy?

No one moves.

JACK: We finished the third act.

No one moves.

JILL: Mommy?
Did you hear Jack?
He said we finished the third act.

JILL goes to WALT.

JILL: Will you watch it, Daddy?

WALT swallows hard.

He nods.

WALT: Does it have a name, Jilly Bean?

JILL: It does!
It does have a name.
It's really hard to say, Daddy.

Jack?

How do you say it again?

JACK: Et tu, Brute.

JILL: That's it!

It's called Hettoo Bootay, Daddy!

WALT: That's wonderful, Little Bean.

You're very clever.

I really don't know where you get it.

I really don't.

WALT eyes BARB who is fixated on a particularly warm, fleshy spot on his back.

JILL: Are you ready, Daddy?

Mommy?

BARB: Oh, I'm ready.

WALT: We're ready, Bean.

JILL: Hooray!

Hit it Jack!

JACK begins to yodel.

Maybe he is quite good.

If he is not, that's fine, too.

JILL is definitely not good.

She yodels like a little girl who is trying to yodel.

JACK: YODEL-AY-EE-AY-EE-AY-EE!

YODEL-AY-EE-OOOOOH!

JILL: YODEL-AY-EE-OOOOOH!

JACK: YODEL-AY-EE-AY-EE-OOOOOH!

JACK hits play on the stereo.

Some music comes on.

Something very upbeat like "Ich Wünsch Mir Einen Jodler" would be perfect.

Something about three whole minutes long.

If you can stretch it longer, do it.

JILL goes to JACK.

They hold hands and do a dance.

It is very stylized.

They kick and twirl in unison.

They cartwheel.

And flip.

And skip.

They walk on their hands.

Lots of big smiles.

Halfway through the song, JACK hits JILL on the head.

It's all part of the dance.

She pretends to strangle him.

He pretends to die.

Then he hops up.

They shrug.

They dance wilder!

Faster!

They chase each other around the room

And finish with a big trick and a pose!

WALT starts to clap, but eyes BARB and changes his mind.

Silence.

JACK: Well.

What did you think?

JILL: Mommy?

WALT: Mommy loved it, Bean.

    We both did.

JACK: Come on.

    They don't give a shit, Jill.

JILL: Jack!

JACK crosses his arms and pouts.

JACK: Come on.

    Let's go finish.

    We're almost done.

    Only one more act.

JILL: Daddy?

WALT and BARB stare at each other.

JILL: Daddy?

    I'm afraid.

WALT: Of what, Jilly?

JILL: Daddy.

    I love you.

    I love you, Daddy!

WALT: And I love you, Beanie.

    Beanie Weenie.

    Now go play with Jack.

JACK: Come on.

JACK and JILL run out.

A suspended moment.

WALT: What a silly play.

Silence.

WALT: These kids.

Silence.

WALT: You know.

What *does* it mean?

Silence.

BARB: Walt.

When we met, do you know what I thought?

My exact thought.

"I have such hope for him."

All my hope is inside the shell of this man, now.

Or boy, rather.

There was no point in undoing it.

As though something was sucked out of me and thrown into you.

You had me.

You were a poet, Walt!

You really were.

You said beautiful things.

Beautiful beautiful.

Things I so desired to say.

Words I don't have.

But where have you gone?

You are like the mist of your former self.

If that!

That former self is living in someone else's house, I think.

And here is this pile of flesh that sits and consumes and rants.

You *consume*, Walt.

And now I am a thorn to you?

What happens to people to change them this way?

It must have been quiet.

I didn't even notice it.

BARB places the knife on the table.

She slides the toast in front of him.

BARB: Have a bite of my toast, Walt.

And then

A very long silence.

WALT looks at the toast.

He looks at the knife.

He reaches for the knife.

BARB gets it first.

BARB: You fucking swine!

She rakes the knife along his throat, again.

Deeper this time.

A long ribbon of blood flies across the stage.

He stands, holding his neck, gagging.

She stabs him twice in the stomach.

Each time, blood flies.

A lot of blood.

He falls to his knees, choking, bleeding.

BARB: Why didn't you just eat my toast, Walt?

Would it have been that hard to eat my toast?

I made it with such love.

I thought it was love.

Was it love?

I can't remember.

THEY ARE THINGS LIKE THIS THAT I THINK
ABOUT, DEAR.

But then again, they're such stupid thoughts.

Because I'm so stupid, Walt.

And you married so beneath you.

She rolls him over.

BARB: You're so sorry you married me, Walt.

Poor Walt.

Poor old Walt.

He had such aspirations!

And now you have to live with me, Walt.

And you're so sorry you married me.

Here!

I have an idea.

I'll just take care of that real quick, Walt.

WALT is on his back.

BARB stands on his right arm.

She reaches down to his left arm.

BARB: Let's cut out the cancer, shall we, dear?

With the knife, she saws off his ring finger.

He wails.

She holds up the finger.

BARB: Ah!

Much better, dear.

Much, much better, dear.

Even I feel the relief.

She drops his finger down the disposal.

She runs the water.

BARB: Say bye-bye, dear.

He moans.

The disposal roars.

BARB leans back in ecstasy and lets out a long sigh.

BARB: Much better.

Isn't that better, dear?

WALT mumbles something.

BARB: What was that, Walt?

He mumbles again.

BARB: You have to speak up, dear.

If you *want* me to listen.

I'm happy to listen, dear.

What did you say?

WALT: *(With difficulty.)* I said.

You fucking

Bitch.

BARB: Come again, dear?

WALT: You

Fucking

Bitch.

You cock-sucking

PIG.

BARB: There you go, dear!

Let it all out!

WALT: FUUUUCK!

Oh, Jesus, Jesus.

BARB: I pity you, Walt.

I really do.

All this could have been avoided if you had just eaten my toast.

If you had just taken a tiny bite of my toast.

Why was that so hard for you, dear?

Why?

I really want to know.

You who provide twelve meals a day.

Our personal lord and savior.

No, *better* than Jesus, didn't you say?

Didn't you say that, Walt?

But Jesus would have eaten my toast.

JESUS MOTHERFUCKING CHRIST would have eaten my toast.

Why couldn't you have taken a bite?

One bite!

One bite?!

Is that so much to ask?

One swallow!

One mouthful!

ONE FUCKING BITE ONE GODDAMN BITE!

She roars and stabs him again in the side.

Blood flies.

He rolls over.

He crawls a little.

He reaches for the towel.

BARB: Let me help you, dear.

Would you like a towel?

He nods.

She holds up the towel.

BARB: This towel?

He nods.

BARB: Are you sure you want this one, dear?

He nods.

He begins to cry.

BARB: Oh, now.

Here come the waterworks.

She goes to him.

She dabs at his tears with the towel.

BARB: Now, now, Walt.

    Don't cry.

    Don't cry, dear.

    You can't let your emotions take control.

    You really mustn't let them take control.

    She cradles his chin in her hand.

    She smiles at him.

    He cries less.

BARB: Let's have a smile, dear.

    I'll trade you *this* towel

    For *one* little smile.

    Can you smile, dear?

    He nods.

BARB: Let's see it.

    He cries.

BARB: Now, that's not it, dear.

    We both know that's not a smile.

    What will make you smile, Walt?

    What does make you smile?

    I bet Kathy Parkinson makes you smile, Walt.

    I bet she can make you smile.

    He smiles.

    BARB smiles back.

BARB: I wonder what did happen to poor little Timmy.

    WALT smiles more.

    With teeth.

BARB: See?

    That's not too hard.

And now you can have this towel.

Let me just dampen it.

She takes the towel to the sink.

She turns on the water, looks at him, and soaks the towel.

He begins to cry again.

He wails like an animal.

She turns off the water and brings him the wet towel.

BARB: Here you are, dear.

Here's your towel.

Don't you want it, dear?

She rubs his face with the soaked towel.

He sobs hard, angry sobs.

He grabs the towel from her.

BARB: Shhh.

There, there, dear.

You know what's wrong?

You must be hungry!

That must be it, dear.

This lovely Sunday is just passing us by and you haven't had a bite to eat, yet.

Your blood must be going down!

She grabs the plate of blueberry toast.

She picks it up and flies it in front of him like an airplane.

BARB: Whooosh!

Here you are!

Breakfast!

How about one little bite?

Just one bite, dear?

Zoom!

Zoom!

Zoom!

Here comes the compote!

WALT's sobs become screeches.

He finds some hidden strength.

He throws the towel around BARB's neck.

He chokes her.

BARB gasps for breath.

He pulls her up by the neck.

He grabs the toast with one hand.

He smears blueberry compote all over her face.

WALT: You eat the toast!

You eat the fucking toast, you whore!

YOU FUCKING BEAST!

He shoves his fingers into her mouth.

She gags on blueberry compote.

She spits it up.

He releases her.

She crawls away.

He grabs her by the hair and pulls her back.

She crawls away again.

She stands.

She goes for the knife.

He stands, slowly.

He backhands her.

Blood flies from her nose.

He grabs another piece of toast.

He forces her mouth open.

He shoves the toast into her mouth.

She chokes on it.

He stands and goes to the kitchen.

He looks around for something.

He grabs a meat tenderizer.

He runs to strike her with it.

She ducks.

She grabs the knife.

He runs to strike her again.

He hits her in the back of the head.

Blood flies everywhere.

She groans and falls.

She wails.

WALT stumbles.

He begins to lose his strength.

He falls to his knees.

They both roll around for a minute.

Then BARB rises.

WALT sees her and rises.

They face each other.

They both scream like wild monkeys.

They howl like dogs.

They fly at each other.

BARB stabs WALT in the stomach.

He falls.

She stabs him over and over and over.

So much blood.

A waterfall of blood.

WALT is still.

BARB is splattered in red.

She stands.

She goes to the sink and turns on the water.

She washes her hands.

After a while, she laughs.

She roars.

She goes to the trash and digs.

She pulls out a plate of blueberry toast.

She arranges it nicely.

She sets it on the table.

She smiles.

She touches the wound on her head.

A flap of skin has come off.

BARB: Oh, dear.

WALT groans.

BARB: Oh.

Are you still with us, Walt?
We thought that you had left.

He groans.

BARB: Speak up, dear.

He groans.

He begins to crawl.

BARB: Mmm-hmm.

Magnificent thought, Walt.

Spoken like a real something.

He crawls slowly across the room.

He trails blood.

BARB watches him.

BARB: Are you going somewhere, dear?

Going over to the Parkinsons, I assume?

Well.

I'm afraid you might not make it today.

You just might not make it today, dear.

I'll call Kathy and apologize.

Send Timmy our best.

WALT manages to crawl to the other side of the room.

He crawls off.

He disappears.

BARB: You're just going to make it faster, dear.

But then again, you *want* to meet your maker.

Show him all your gifts and talents or something.

Tell him about all the horrible Unitarians and the WOMEN.

She laughs hysterically.

BARB: Walt?

Did you make it to heaven yet, Walt?

She laughs.

BARB: Save me a place at the RIGHT HAND, Walt!

Walt?

The RIGHT HAND!

She laughs.

BARB: Since you already lost a bit of your

She laughs.

BARB: Walt?

Silence.

BARB: I have some COMPOTE here.

It's very MOIST!

Silence.

BARB: Dear?

She sighs.

She sits for a while.

A long, lonely silence.

Eventually, she touches the back of her head.

It hurts.

She goes to the sink and dampens a towel.

She checks the back of her head in the stainless steel refrigerator.

She touches the towel to her head.

It stings.

She winces.

She uses the dry end instead.

She tries to reattach the flap of skin.

She sighs.

She hears a noise.

She turns.

It is WALT.

He has stumbled in.

And he has a gun.

BARB: Walt!

He points the gun at her.

She whimpers.

He shoots her.

Blood splatters all over the refrigerator.

BARB sinks to the floor and dies.

WALT drops the gun.

He falls to the floor.

He doesn't move.

JACK and JILL run in.

JILL gasps.

JILL: Daddy?

Daddy what happened?!

He groans.

JILL: Are you alright, Daddy?

He groans.

JACK: We finished the play.

Would you like to see it?

JILL: It's not long, Daddy.

It's the final act!

This one's called a

What's it called, Jack?

JACK: A soliloquy.

JILL: Right!

A soliloquy, Daddy.

He groans.

JILL: No, it doesn't have a title, Daddy.

JACK: It's Untitled.

JILL: So you can make up the title for yourself.

Isn't that clever?

It was Jack's idea.

He groans.

JILL: Great!

Jack, hit the lights!

JACK hits the lights.

Everything fades to darkness.

A hard spotlight on JILL.

For a minute we have left the kitchen

And JILL is no longer JILL.

JILL: Once upon a time

A little girl was playing by the woods.

It was getting very late and she was getting very hungry.

She came across a pack of wild dogs.

These dogs were foaming at the mouth

And biting each other with their teeth

And fighting over this one little bird that had fallen from a tree above.

This one tiny little bird.

And the little girl stopped in her tracks.

She was so afraid.

She tried to sneak away, but the dogs saw her.

Their eyes lit on fire.

And the little girl knew she had to fight them.

But when she saw their eyes and their hideous jaws

She thought

I am not one of you!

And she turned to go.

But the dogs followed her

So she shouted behind her

I AM NOT ONE OF YOU!

And she ran!

She ran faster and faster!

And they were right on her tail.

So she climbed up into a tree

And they barked and snarled

And she thought

No, I am not one of you.

And she sat in the tree

And ate nuts and berries

Until she was very old.

And then one day a spaceship came and took her away.

The lights shift back.

JACK: That's it.

That's the end of the play.

JILL: Did you like it, Daddy?

Did you think it was a good play?

Silence.

JACK: They don't give a shit, Jill.

JILL: Jack!

JACK: They don't!

Look at them!

JILL: That's not a very nice thing to say.

JACK: It's true.

JILL: Daddy, tell Jack that isn't a nice thing to say!

JACK: Oh, Jill.

Shut the fuck up.

They're *dead*.

JILL: What?!

JACK: Yes, *Jilly Bean*.

They're fucking toast.

So stop whining.

Daddy, Daddy, Daddy!

It's pathetic.

JILL cries.

JILL: But, Jack?

What will we do?

JACK: I don't know!

How the hell am I supposed to know?

JILL weeps.

She touches WALT.

JACK: Please stop crying, Jill.

I hate to see you cry.

She cries harder.

JACK: Please don't cry!

She wails!

JACK: For the love of Christ!

For the love of Christ!

Shut your fucking mouth, Jill!

JACK picks up the gun.

He shoots JILL in the head.

She dies.

JACK drops the gun.

He looks around.

He goes to the table.

He sits in his father's chair.

A long silence.

End of Play.

WWW.OBERONBOOKS.COM